Apprentice Blogger

Learn How to Start A Successful Blog Correctly the First Time

By Macarena Torres

Table of Contents

Getting the Word Out...................41

Brand Identity and its Value for

Business 49

Introduction

Setting up your blog will require a little research and review; you'll need to consider the factors of cost, the time and skills you currently have, and your readiness to learn some new software.

Almost all blog software is very easy to use and offers a variety of plug-ins and other resources to make yours unique. You don't necessarily need to hire a professional or specialist to start publishing; most blogs can be set up with a few hours, and you can learn how to use them as you go.

Below are some of today's leading blog platforms. The three most widely used platforms include:

- WordPress
- Blogger
- TypePad

Choosing the Right Blog Platform for Your Business

You'll find a number of free and low-cost fee-based blog platforms available, and most of them use a simple text editor box for publishing.

The cost differences vary depending on the type of blog you are running; if you are going to host the blog on your own domain, you will need to manage hosting fees. Blogs run within the blog's domain are usually free, but you will not have a simple address to work with.

If you want a unique URL, it's better to consider the different packages, even if you're starting out with the very basic.

Most basic packages allow you to add your own design elements and start making money with advertisements immediately. Most free hosts will not allow advertising, which limits your ability to start generating a separate stream of income from ad clicks and sales. If you're just starting out, it's best to pick the basic version so you can at least start driving traffic to advertisements.

Next, you'll need to consider how much you know about blog design. If you're already proficient with web design and templates, this will be fairly easy, but if you do not know where to start, there are plenty of blog templates available.

Blog templates can help you construct your basic site and then change it later when you need to. These can be easily replaced with a more comprehensive design, but most blog platforms provide a variety of options, colors, and basic attributes to make your blog stand out.

Blog platforms such as WordPress can be very helpful in getting you set up with a professional look, especially if you have limited design skills and are not working with a web or graphic designer immediately.

Blogger also offers customizable options, and you'll find a range of colors and styles to choose from. The moveable type is somewhat limited, but you can still find a basic, well-organized template.

Basics of a Blog Setup

Even though each blog platform has different elements and plug-ins available, you'll need to come up with some ideas for your basic blog setup and structure.

This is comprised of the types and categories of information you intend to share with the audience.

For example, you will need to create content for your:

- Profile page/About Us section
- A contact pages
- Resources
- Blog categories for each type of news
- Deciding whether to accept comments
- Basic marketing elements such as a blogroll or link exchange
- Space for advertising
- Feeds
- Ad Sense sections

- Logos
- Blog archives
- Page headers

After identifying the basic elements of your blog, it's time to choose the actual platform you will be using. It's not a good idea to switch platforms at a later date since you'll probably end up reformatting and editing every piece of content.

Choosing the right fit from the start is the best way to keep things moving along smoothly and simply.

Other Considerations

Another important consideration after setting up your blog is the amount and frequency of your postings. It may be helpful to create a schedule for posting, and almost all blog platforms allow you to set a time and date stamp so you can control when things appear on your blog.

This can be helpful when you want to pull together a batch of posts and release them one by one. Doing this will make sure that your blog is continuously updated, and you can choose to do this once per week, once per day, or even every hour if you want to!

This strategy will help you to plan ahead and provide quality content on a regular basis. Remember that many readers simply subscribe to your blog through the RSS reader, and having something fresh and newly available on a regular basis will help them stay 'in touch.'

You'll also be able to earn recognition from search engines since the crawlers are constantly looking for websites that are constantly updated.

How Your Blog Should Be Organized

Understanding how each element of your blog comes together is essential for the long-term success of your business blog.

After you've gained some experience with using the platform you've chosen, it's a good idea to take a close look at each area and learn what can, and perhaps cannot be, optimized to suit your best.

Besides the visitor traffic counts, the overall structure and pieces of your blog can help to increase exposure.

Do keep in mind that every area of the blog can help your site become more search engine-friendly. Not only does this reduce overall marketing costs when you are trying to obtain search engine rankings, but you'll also start to see more 'organic' traffic simply by tweaking a few areas.

Everything from the blog layout, the template you choose, and the fonts and colors you use will have an impact on your final blog.

You'll want to choose wisely when it comes to each area, especially paying attention to color schemes and other themes that may help with branding purposes.

Layout and Basic Composition

The layout is a part of your blog design, and your goal is to create something that will leave a lasting impression. More and more blog networks are creating 'generic' blogs that have very little creativity and are focused more on the new content instead.

Even though the content of your blog is a critical element, what the visitor sees and feels as they explore your blog is just as important.

If you choose a simple layout and design, just make sure to navigate it yourself and see what your focal point is. Are you focusing too much on the sidebars? Is the header distracting? Can you easily read the content, or do you have to squint to make sense of the font and style?

All of these elements will be unique to your blog, and since it may be an extension of your company and brand, it's vital that you use something that will make a lasting impression.

The blog layout consists of:

- Fonts
- Color themes
- Line spacing
- Header styles
- Image boxes
- Advertising space
- Columns (one-, two-, or three-columns)

Building Social Authority

Establishing credibility is both a short-term and long-term goal for your business blog, and the more valuable information that you provide for your audience, the higher the chances of success.

Today's competitive blogosphere makes it challenging to meet the needs of your target market if you do not pay attention to quality and maintaining some consistent standards as you start posting.

People who are turned off by your blog are less likely to return; with thousands of blogs on similar subjects, it is easy to lose traffic because of a lack of experience, poor writing, or simply not updating your blog enough.
Valuable blogs receive ongoing traffic as they start showing up on directories and indexes across the web.

These include sites such as:

- Technorati
- Daypop
- Blogdex
- Blogstreet
- Digg

All of these directories receive thousands, even millions, of visitors each day. Each item that is listed on the site receives ratings or reviews from other users, and you can start establishing credibility simply by joining.

These sites also contain thousands of articles and topic matter related to your subject; they can serve as effective research tools when you are developing blog content and can give you some valuable links to work with as you start developing fresh ideas.

When your overall site is indexed on these directories in the appropriate category, this also provides some credibility.

People who are searching across these networks can see that your blog may be more worthy of attention, especially when you include a logo, title, or description for the catalog.

Elements for Credibility: What Your Blog MUST Have

There are some essential elements that your blog must have in order to credible.

These are a combination of the site structure and design, as well as the style and type of content you start posting.

Each blog must include:

- Author name and company (if any)
- Contact information
- A brief Bio or About Us section
- Blogroll
- Links to resources
- Well-balanced visual elements
- A steady amount of ads
- No spam in comment boxes
- Compelling language and headlines
- Proper language, free from typos
- References to sources
- Carefully placed affiliate links (if any at all)

- Author responses on comments
- Appropriate language and conduct

You'll start with providing the author's name and company; this is essential for helping your readers make a 'human' connection to your blog, and they should be able to contact you directly with any questions.

Blog readers are looking for an 'insider' perspective on most issues, and it is very helpful for them to be able to distinguish company marketing materials from an actual first-person perspective. Knowing who the author is will help to bring the message of the blog closer to home.

This goes hand-in-hand with the contact information. You can include your e-mail address or even a phone number if necessary.

The goal is to make sure users can trust that the information is coming from a real person, and they have the freedom to contact the author if necessary.

This can help you create a connection with both customers and random visitors, providing credibility for your content.

Next, it's a good idea to provide a brief bio. This can also take the form of an 'About Us' section that briefly summarizes who you are, why the blog exists, and what you plan to include. This can be helpful for anyone who simply stumbles across the blog and needs a quick summary of what your blog is about.

This information may also be included on the homepage, as it can help direct users to the appropriate resources–your main website, for example—instead.

The blogroll is a very effective marketing tool, as it helps readers see who else is linking to your blog and where to find more information.

The blogroll is your connection to other blogs in the blogosphere, and credible blogs listed here will, in turn, help you earn some credibility. A blogroll should be comprised of at least ten to fifteen different blogs or websites.

It's a good idea to send out e-mails to everyone on the blogroll notifying them of the inclusion and hopefully listing you on their blogroll as well. This will help boost traffic from other resources while helping you link up to some valuable blogs for referencing as well.

The Resource Links section is another area that will demonstrate credibility; a solid resource list will inform your readers that you are using various resources for research and keeping up to date with news in your industry, and also provide them with other navigation options as they browse your site.

The resources links section can also be followed up with an e-mail to each website notifying them of the inclusion. They may choose to participate in a link exchange program. As a result, furthering your chances of increased traffic.

Blog Credibility and SEO

Search engines today are becoming even more refined and smarter at finding relevant and informative sites and blogs to index, and your blog will receive a higher credibility status when it encompasses most of the important elements.

Search engines and directories are looking for:

- Relevant content
- Appropriate formatting and titles
- Steady visitor traffic
- Linking in from other sites
- Regular posting and updating
- Consistency in blog content
- Sites free of spam and excessive advertising
- Effective use of Ad Sense

How Visitors Determine Credibility

Making yourself a trustworthy and credible resource on the web takes time but becoming an expert in your niche industry is an essential step towards the regular readership.

Even if your blog is an extension of your website, you can use it as a subsidiary resource platform that can help introduce readers to your company and encourage them to continue reading.

From the customer or visitor's perspective, there are essential signs of credibility that help distinguish one source from another.

This includes:

Longevity of The Blog

How long has it been active, how many posts are there?

Experience

Does the author have other sites and experience published around the web? If so, what are they? Expertise – can the author verify their expertise?

Design

Is the site well-constructed and updated according to industry standards?

Writing Style

Is the author a strong writer, or do they seem to post poorly written content on a regular basis?

Readership

Has the blog or site reached a high amount of readers? Many people turn to ranking indexes such as Alexa to determine this.

Consistency

Are the posts regular and arranged in the appropriate categories, or are they simply submitted to the blog randomly?

Transparency

Is the voice natural and friendly, or does it sound like it is coming from the marketing/PR department of the company?

Gaining steady readership will take time, but establishing credibility is a long-term goal for any blogger, regardless of experience.

Knowing how to convey a message that catches your reader's interest is a necessary step; take the time to research, review, and edit your blog posts each time and make sure that the overall blog setup and design are in line with the competition.

Getting the Word Out

Earning blog credibility, increasing traffic, and promoting your blog in the process are all part of your marketing strategy.

The only way you can build your brand is by becoming highly visible across a variety of domains; this includes blogging communities, social networking groups, and even discussion forums where your target market can be found on a regular basis.

Marketing and branding go hand in hand with your company website, and even more so if your blog is the only online entity of your business.

There are a number of ways to develop a cohesive marketing strategy as you shift into the online world; this involves:

- Developing relationships with other bloggers.

- Identifying top blogging communities.
- Determining a brand identity and tracking its impact on your business.

Developing Relationships with Other Bloggers

No matter what type of visitor reaches your site—from the average guest to another blogger in your industry—there are many ways you can develop an ongoing relationship.

Relationships are important in both the online and offline world, and a successful blog is often based on the first impression. Making sure you've taken the time to invest in site design and layout can help considerably with attracting a large audience.

A blog can make a good first impression when it is:

- Easy to read
- Easy to navigate
- Provides useful and timely content
- It is built with categories and organized appropriately
- Offers archives filled with keyword content (easily indexed by search engines)
- Offers related posts
- Is consistent

Always remember that the blog represents your brand and is a virtual representation of your company. Communicating with your visitors and readers regularly involves your content, and understanding what they may be interested in reading will help you develop quality postings.

When you are looking for fresh content to share, working with other bloggers will give you a chance to reach out beyond your scope of knowledge and make use of all of your resources.

Top Blogging Communities

Participating in blogging communities will ensure that you are deeply networked with other bloggers and will help you increase your visibility as well.

Blogging communities are rapidly growing across the web, but knowing which ones to join can be a challenge.

Some communities are simply not a valuable use of your time, and you can spend hours participating in discussions and comments with little or no traffic increases.

A few blogging communities that can help you grow your business, however, do exist.

You may try setting up profiles on:

- MyBlogLog
- Blogger
- WordPress Groups
- Google Groups
- Facebook Groups

Brand Identity and its Value for Business

Your blog serves as your virtual 'branding stamp' and can help your business or company gain visibility far more easily than even direct marketing.

The more involved and well-linked you are within your industry, the higher the chances of you gaining visibility, traffic, and ongoing readers.

Developing readership and subscribers is a valuable goal for any blog, especially when you are building one as an extension of an already-established website.

Blogs are becoming more and more interactive and acceptable to visitors; instead of shying away from websites that are full of advertising, more people are showing interested in specialized niches presented on a blog.

Using this to your advantage is vital for enhancing your brand, and the more credibility you have, the higher your rate of success.

Customers and consumers that identify with your brand will have a unique set of expectations for items that you develop and promote.

Making sure that your blog is aligned with your company's values, mission statement, and overall design will be in your best interest for building an audience.

Marketing and promoting your blog with this in mind can be the key to a successful marketing strategy and one that simply gets lost in the growing blogosphere.

Summary of Marketing Essentials for Promoting Your Blog

Now that you've covered the key elements of promoting, social networking, and joining blog communities, it may be helpful to reduce the concepts down for a summary.

Here are the marketing essentials for promoting your blog; combining at least eight to nine of these as a basis for your first marketing effort will help you get ahead and start promoting your blog with much higher chances of success:

Post-High-Quality Content on A Regular Basis

If you are providing news on your site, average post amounts range from 3-5 posts per day. Make the most of your postings by only posting unique and high-quality content. If you are looking to entertain or engage readers, aim for at least one posting per day.

Enable Automatic Trackbacks and Pinging

Pings are a valuable way to notify search engines that your blog has been updated. Increase the chances of sharing blog content by enabling trackbacks on your blog.

Make Sure All Posts Are Formatted and Archived Correctly

When you first start out, it can be helpful to leave this as a future project until you have developed some solid content. After that, take the time to sort through your content and make sure it is placed in the appropriate category.

Also, keep in mind that categories need to be based on keywords; you can gain a significant advantage with the search engines when you include high-ranking keywords in your category section.

Develop Your Own Link Building Campaign

Whether this involves contacting other bloggers, responding to comments and providing linkbacks, or simply making a 'call out' for links as you post, make sure you are keeping track of results and try a variety of strategies.

Make Sure Your Blog Is Optimized

Template optimization involves the URLS, RSS subscription buttons, and title tags are embedded appropriately. While most blogging platforms can help you do this automatically, you will need to pay attention to these areas on an ongoing basis.

Submit Any Podcasts and Media Files to The Appropriate Directories

If you do start developing podcasts for your blog, make sure you are submitting them to the appropriate directories. Most are free and can help you gain even higher rankings on the search engines.

Comment on Other Blogs to Develop Expertise

Researching is just as important as writing for your blog, and you can search other blogs relevant to your industry and start commenting appropriately.

Keep in mind the rules of the forum or group, and make sure your posts are relevant to the discussion. Always remember that your credibility is an important part of this, so be resourceful and post accordingly.

Develop A Glossary Section

This is an often-overlooked opportunity for increasing search engine rankings and can be a valuable resource section for your readers as well.

A glossary can be as simple as keywords with definitions, and you can also start inter-linking the definitions to actual posts within your blog.

Customize Your Blog and Design It with Your Logo in Mind

Even if you aren't launching with an exact replica of your website colors, choose something similar that will be attractive to your readers.

Customized designs and templates are the best way to make a valuable first impression, but you may choose to wait until a later date.

Setup A Google Sitemap

Google sitemaps are designed to capture the key elements of your blog and validate them for search engines. This is one valuable step toward web optimization and can significantly impact search engine rankings.

Identify A-List of Authoritative Blogs and Other Web Sites

Even if you are not using these on your blogroll or link exchange program, knowing where to consult information can help you develop content on a regular basis. Create a comprehensive list of at least 15-20 sites that can help you post unique and relevant content.

Make Use of Statistics

Statistics will help you track results and easily see fluctuations in visitor traffic. Most blog platforms are equipped with statistical analysis programs, and you can watch trends and patterns daily.

Promote Yourself on Social Networking Platforms

These are essential for gaining exposure and a strong presence alongside your target market, and you can join different groups and communities very easily.

Setting up the right profile will take some strategy (see Chapter 7) but is an important element of building your social community presence.

Submit Links to Social Bookmarking Sites

This is a very effective way to promote individual pieces of content. As soon as you have created a URL of your submission, that link can be promoted across multiple channels and networks in just a few steps.

Try submitting to the major social bookmarking sites such as Technorati, Digg, and StumbleUpon for increased exposure on highly valuable topics and content.

Even interacting on these networks can help you learn what types of content and topics your audience may be looking for.

Position Yourself as An Authority

Consult valuable resources and give appropriate credit on your blog. This is not only helpful for your readers but can help you establish yourself as an expert within your field.

Focus on Building Credibility

You can build credibility by communicating directly with other bloggers in the industry, establish a guest blogging opportunity for other bloggers to participate, and encourage them to market their contributions in the process.

Make Contact with Bloggers Offline as Well

You can still build credibility and enjoy networking in the offline world and attract some new visitors the 'traditional way.

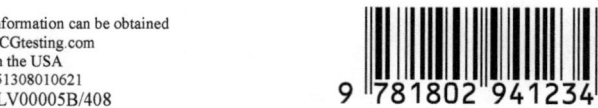